explaining why things happen the way they do in nature. For an idea to be accepted as a scientific theory, most scientists must agree with it. Plate tectonics helps explain many things, such as why earthquakes happen and how mountains form.

All of Earth's land and water are on its plates. Plate tectonics explains how these plates move.

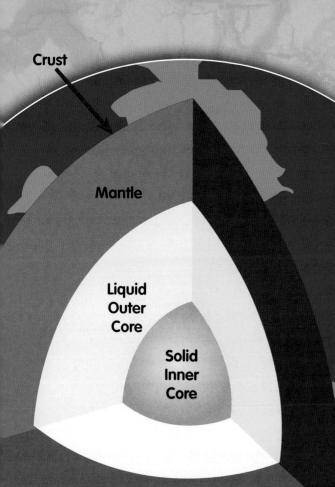

Crust

Mantle

Liquid
Outer
Core

Solid
Inner
Core

Like an onion, Earth has layers. The outside layer is the **crust**. It is about 3 miles (5 km) thick under oceans and 19 miles (30 km) thick under land. The crust is made up of fairly light rock. It floats on the heavier rock of the **mantle** below it. The mantle is about 100 times thicker than the crust. Some of its rock is hot and liquid.

This drawing shows Earth's layers. The inner core is the hottest layer. The layers get colder as you move out from the core.

Much of the rock in Earth's crust is in layers, too. It is easy to see these layers in certain places, such as Quebrada de Humahuaca, Argentina.

Earth's plates are made up of the crust and the top part of the mantle.

Beneath the mantle is the **core**. The core has two parts. The outer core is made of liquid metal. The inner core is solid metal.

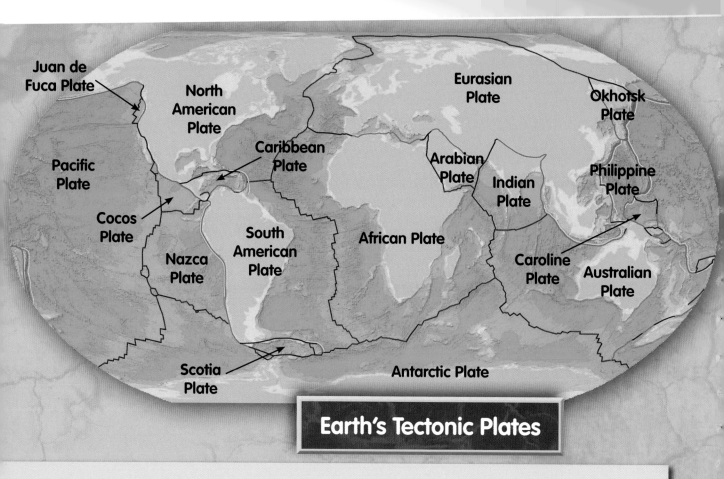

Juan de Fuca Plate

North American Plate

Eurasian Plate

Okhotsk Plate

Pacific Plate

Caribbean Plate

Arabian Plate

Philippine Plate

Cocos Plate

Indian Plate

Nazca Plate

South American Plate

African Plate

Caroline Plate

Australian Plate

Scotia Plate

Antarctic Plate

Earth's Tectonic Plates

Plates come in many shapes and sizes. A plate can hold water, land, or both. The Antarctic plate stretches out under the Southern Ocean and parts of several other oceans. The plate also holds the **continent** of Antarctica. Continents are Earth's biggest landmasses.

Some plates have more than one continent on them. The North American plate has not only North America, but also part of Russia. Most of Russia is on the Eurasian plate, though.

Plates can be very small. The Juan de Fuca plate is one of the smallest. It collides with the North American plate near Washington State. It holds only ocean.

San Diego, California, is on the Pacific plate. Though all of California is part of the continent of North America, parts of southern California are on the Pacific plate.

Plates move very slowly. They move even slower than the rate at which your fingernails grow. Why do they move at all? Scientists do not yet understand all the reasons. They have some ideas, though.

One of their ideas involves heat. Hot, liquid rock called **magma** rises from deep inside Earth. At the surface, it cools off and hardens. The older rock already there sinks down and

Gravity is the force that pulls you back toward Earth when you jump. Without gravity, jumping would make you float off into space!

Melted rock is known as magma when it is inside Earth. When melted rock spills out over Earth's surface, as it is doing here, it is called lava.

melts again. **Gravity**, the force that pulls us toward Earth, pulls the heavy, old rock down into the magma. These forces cause a circular motion that moves the plates.

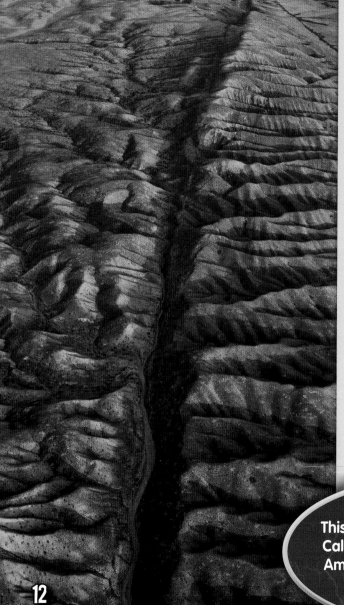

Several things can happen where plates meet. Sometimes magma rises up in between two plates. New rock forms when the magma cools off. The new rock pushes the plates apart. This often happens on the ocean floor.

Sometimes, plates slide past each other. This is happening in California, where the Pacific plate is moving north while the North American plate is moving south.

This is the San Andreas Fault, in California. It is where the North American plate and the Pacific plate meet.

Plates also crash into each other. Today, the Nazca plate is crashing very slowly into the South American plate. Part of the Nazca plate is melting down back into Earth. The crash also crumples up Earth's crust to create mountains.

Iceland's Thingvellir National Park sits on the line between the North American plate and the Eurasian plate. These plates are slowly pulling away from each other.

Many of Earth's landforms were shaped by plate tectonics. When two plates carrying continents crash together, mountains may rise. The Himalayas, in Asia, formed this way. They are still growing today because the Indian plate continues to push against the Eurasian plate.

Sometimes plate tectonics pulls plates apart. Today, magma is rising up to the surface in northeast Africa. It pushes two parts of Africa away from each other. This area is called the Rift Valley. As part of Africa breaks away, a new plate is being formed. In time, water will fill the gap between the plates and form a new ocean.

The Himalayas are Earth's tallest mountains. They grow at a rate of about .5 inch (1 cm) each year.

VOLCANOES AND EARTHQUAKES

Many of Earth's **volcanoes** are found where two plates meet. Volcanoes are places where melted rock spills out of Earth. When one plate melts under another, it forms hot magma. Sometimes the magma rises back up to feed volcanoes. The Juan de Fuca plate is going under the North American plate. It feeds magma to volcanoes, such as Mount St. Helens, in Washington.

The volcano Stromboli rises out of the Mediterranean Sea. It sits over one of the points where the African plate crashes into the Eurasian plate.

Plate movement also causes earthquakes. When two plates move past each other, they sometimes get stuck. They push against each other. When they come unstuck, their sudden movement shakes the ground. This has happened several times in California where the Pacific and North American plates rub together.

Earthquakes under oceans can cause huge waves called tsunamis. In March 2011, an earthquake in the Pacific Ocean set off a tsunami that caused many problems in Japan.

Have you ever looked at a map and noticed that South America and Africa would fit together like two puzzle pieces? It looks like that because they really were joined together once!

This map shows Earth as it looked about 200 million years ago, when Pangaea started to break up.

PLATE TECTONICS

Jason D. Nemeth

PowerKiDS
press

New York

Published in 2012 by The Rosen Publishing Group, Inc.
29 East 21st Street, New York, NY 10010

First Edition

Editor: Amelie von Zumbusch
Book Design: Greg Tucker

Photo Credits: Cover, pp. 4, 5, 6, 7, 10, 13, 14–15, 16, 20, 21, 22 Shutterstock.com; p. 8 Dorling Kindersley/Getty Images; p. 9 Comstock/Thinkstock; p. 11 Stockbyte/Thinkstock; p. 12 Baron Wolman/Getty Images; p. 17 Kim Kyung-Hoon/AFP/Getty Images; p. 18 Mikkel Juul Jensen/ Bonnier Publications/Photo Researchers, Inc.; p. 19 Ken Lucas/Getty Images.

Library of Congress Cataloging-in-Publication Data

Nemeth, Jason D.
 Plate tectonics / by Jason D. Nemeth. — 1st ed.
   p. cm. — (Our changing earth)
 Includes index.
 ISBN 978-1-4488-6168-2 (library binding) — ISBN 978-1-4488-6294-8 (pbk.) —
ISBN 978-1-4488-6295-5 (6-pack)
 1. Plate tectonics—Juvenile literature. I. Title.
 QE511.4.N46 2012
 551.1'36—dc23

                                    2011022772

Manufactured in the United States of America

CPSIA Compliance Information: Batch #WW12PK: For Further Information contact Rosen Publishing, New York, New York at 1-800-237-9932

CONTENTS

JIGSAW EARTH

North America's Rocky Mountains were formed by plate tectonics.

Scientists believe that Earth's surface is like a giant puzzle. It is made up of pieces called **plates**. These plates are huge slabs of rock. They fit together closely. All of Earth's land and the oceans sit on top of them.

The **scientific theory** that describes how these plates work is called **plate tectonics**. A scientific theory is a way of

Pangaea and the waters around it were home to many animals that are no longer living, such as *Keichousaurus*. The remains of two of these swimming reptiles are shown here.

Scientists think that all the continents were pressed together to make one big **supercontinent** about 225 million years ago. They call this Pangaea, which means "all lands."

As plates moved, Pangaea slowly began to break apart. The land that is now North America, Europe, and Asia broke away to create a continent called Laurasia. What is now Africa, South America, Australia, and Antarctica formed Gondwana. The plates kept moving to create the world we know today.

For many centuries, people believed that Earth's crust was unchanging. **Evidence**, or proof, for plate tectonics came in the 1950s and 1960s. Scientists discovered mountain ranges on the seafloor in the middle of the Atlantic Ocean. The rocks of these mountains were not

The remains of living things also hold clues about Earth's past. Scientists in India found the remains of animals that looked like the lemurs that live in Madagascar today. This made them wonder if the lands were once joined.

as old as rocks near the coasts. This showed that magma was rising and creating new crust.

If new crust was being made, then old crust must be disappearing. If not, Earth would just keep getting bigger. Then scientists found ocean trenches where one plate sinks beneath another. This offered more proof for plate tectonics.

One reason people started looking at the seafloor in the 1960s was because they hoped to drill for oil there. What they found offered evidence for plate tectonics, too!

WHERE ARE EARTH'S PLATES HEADED?

Earth's plates will keep moving until there is no more heat inside Earth. Scientists have some ideas about how they will fit together in the years to come.

In 10 million years, Los Angeles and San Francisco, California, will be next to each other. In 100 million years, Africa will be connected to Europe. In 250 million years, there will likely be another supercontinent. Yet even that will break up again as Earth's plates continue to move and change.

Plate tectonics is making the Atlantic Ocean wider. The plates underneath it push apart at a rate of about 1 inch (2.5 cm) each year.

GLOSSARY

continent (KON-tuh-nent) One of Earth's large landmasses.

core (KOR) The hot center of Earth.

crust (KRUST) The outside of a planet.

evidence (EH-vuh-dunts) Facts that prove something.

gravity (GRA-vih-tee) The natural force that causes objects to move toward the center of Earth.

magma (MAG-muh) Hot, melted rock inside Earth.

mantle (MAN-tel) The middle layer of Earth.

plates (PLAYTS) The moving pieces of Earth's crust, the top layer of Earth.

plate tectonics (PLAYT tek-TAH-niks) The study of the moving pieces of Earth's crust.

scientific theory (sy-en-TIH-fik THEE-uh-ree) An idea or group of ideas that tries to explain something in the natural world.

supercontinent (SOO-per-kon-tuh-nent) A huge landmass made up of several of today's continents.

volcanoes (vol-KAY-nohz) Openings that sometimes shoots up hot, melted rock called lava.

INDEX

WEB SITES

Due to the changing nature of Internet links, PowerKids Press has developed an online list of Web sites related to the subject of this book. This site is updated regularly. Please use this link to access the list:
www.powerkidslinks.com/chng/plate/